DICTIONARY
OF PREPOSITIONS
FOR STUDENTS OF ENGLISH

EUGENE J. HALL

MINERVA BOOKS, LTD.
30 West 26th Street, New York, NY 10010

ESL CENTER

Illustrations by Barbara Camhi

Published by

MINERVA BOOKS, LTD.

30 West 26th Street
New York, NY 10010

PRINTED IN THE UNITED STATES OF AMERICA

ISBN: 0-8056-0114-7

INTRODUCTION

Prepositions are classed as function words in discussions of grammar; that is, they fill a grammatical function or purpose. The auxiliary verbs which are used to form most English verb phrases are also function words. The particular function of a preposition is to relate a noun, a pronoun, or a verb form used as a noun to another part of a sentence. The preposition can relate a noun to a verb:

We talked *about the weather*.

It can relate one noun to another noun:

I read a book *about the stars*.

It can also relate a noun to an adjective:

She's happy *about her promotion*.

A preposition with its object (the word or expression that follows it) is called a prepositional phrase. The object of a preposition is always a noun, a pronoun, or a verb form used as a noun.

She asked me *about the memorandum*.

I forgot to send her a copy *of it*.

She walked away *without speaking to me*.

The object of the preposition can have any or all of its usual modifiers.

They live *in a big house*.

They live *in the big house on the hill*.

They live *in the big house on the hill that they bought last year*.

The verb form that follows a preposition is usually the present participle, the *-ing* form of the verb.

I've been thinking *about studying physics*.

You can depend *on my finishing this job today*.

Note that in the second sentence, *finishing* has its own subject (*my*), its own object (*this job*), and an adverbial modifier of time (*today*).

The only exception is *to* when it serves as the sign of the infinitive; in this case, *to* is followed by the simple form of the verb.

I want *to read* that book.

Prepositions are single words like *about*, *to*, and *before*. They also include several phrases that act as prepositions—*because of*, *in case of*, and *in addition to*, for example. Many of the single-word prepositions are among the most common words in English. Such prepositions as *to*, *at*, *in*, *on*, *with*, *by*, *for*, and *from* are high on all the frequency counts that have been made on the vocabulary of English. Many prepositions, particularly those that refer to directions, like *up*, *down*, *over*, *under*, also act as adverbs.

I climbed *up the stairs.*

I'm going *up to see the director.*

In the first sentence, *up* is a preposition followed by a noun. In the second sentence, *up* is not followed by a noun and therefore acts as an adverb.

Prepositions act as function words, but like the modal auxiliary verbs (*may*, *can*, *should*, etc.), they also have meanings. Indeed, some of the more common prepositions have many different meanings. Sometimes a preposition, *with*, for example, has meanings that are almost opposite.

I had a fight *with my brother.* (I fought against him.)

I'm going to stick *with my brother*, no matter what happens. (I'm going to support him.)

This book is intended to help students of English learn the different uses of the prepositions. It lists 115 prepositions or phrases that act as prepositions. A definition is given for each different meaning of the preposition, and this is followed by one or more examples of the use of the preposition in that meaning. In some cases, a particular meaning is further clarified by an illustration. A few archaic prepositions—*anent*, *ere*, *saving*, and *unto*, for example—have been omitted. Also, a few of the longer and stylistically more awkward phrases—*in the event of* and *as a result of*, for example—have not been included.

Students of English must learn to understand and use the prepositions. This book is offered in the hope that it will make that task easier.

a

a/an

A and *an* are the indefinite articles, used to designate a singular noun that has not previously been identified. They are also used as prepositions before expressions of time or measurement to mean *for each one.*

> We have six classes *a day.*
> That material costs ten dollars *a yard.*

A is used before words that begin with a consonant sound, and *an* is used before words that begin with a vowel sound.

> She can type sixty words *a minute.*
> The speed limit is fifty-five miles *an hour.*

aboard/on board

Aboard and *on board* are almost always used before a form of transportation to indicate that something is on or in it.

> We met each other *aboard ship.*
> All the passengers are *aboard the train* now.
> They're loading the crates *on board the truck* now.

about

About is a common preposition with several different uses. One of the most frequent is to indicate the subject of a conversation, etc.

> They've been talking *about their problems.*
> He thought *about his homework*, but he didn't do it.

In a similar sense, it indicates something connected with or related to.

> We haven't received any information *about her plans.*
> I just read an interesting book *about space exploration.*

About also has the meaning of *on all sides of*.

If you look *about you*, you'll see everything you need.

With verbs of motion, **about** indicates movement in an indefinite or uncertain direction, here and there.

She was walking restlessly *about the room*.

In a similar sense, **about** indicates the presence of something or someone at an indefinite place.

I left my briefcase somewhere *about the house*.

above

Above means *higher than*.

The plane was flying *above the clouds*.
There's a light *above my head*.
The moon was directly *above the top of the mountain*.

In a similar sense, **above** also means *superior to*.

Her intelligence is *above average*.
Our boss is not *above helping out* when we're busy.
He wouldn't lie; he's *above that*.

Above is also used to mean *more than*.

My baggage was *above the weight limit*, so I had to pay an extra charge for it.

according to

According to means *as stated by, as shown by*.

According to a friend of mine in personnel, we're all going to get a raise on the first of the month.
According to the map, we should be near the highway now.

According to also means *in agreement with* or *in conformity to*.

She has always tried to act *according to the highest standards of her profession*.

The plane was flying *above the clouds*.

Still another meaning of **according to** is *in proportion to*.

They'll charge you *according to the weight of the shipment*.

on account of

On account of is one of several expressions that are used to state reason or cause.

He had to resign *on account of his health*. (The reason or cause of his resignation was his health.)
They've raised their prices *on account of higher labor costs*.

across

Across is a preposition of place that means *on the other side of*.

There's a grocery store *across the street* from the drugstore.
There are a lot of farms *across the river*.
The desert begins just *across that line of hills*.

Across also means *from one side to the other*.

We had to stop because there was a tree *across the road*.
They're building a new bridge *across the river*.

Across is also used with verbs of motion in the same sense, that is, *from one side to the other*.

I walk *across the bridge* every morning to get to work.
We always cut *across the field* on our way to the park; it's faster that way.

Across is also used in several expressions that indicate meeting or finding something or someone, usually by chance.

She came *across some valuable old books* in the attic.
I ran *across an old friend of mine* at the airport.
He happened *across some interesting facts* while he was reading that article.

Another meaning of **across** is *concerning all the people or groups, especially within a business or industry*.

Management increased salaries *across the board*; everyone got a raise.

I walk *across the bridge* every morning to get to work.

in addition to

In addition to is one of several prepositions or phrases that express the idea of one thing added to another.

She studied chemistry *in addition to physics*.
They've given me a special job *in addition to my regular duties*.

after

After occurs most frequently as a preposition of time to indicate a later time than.

She had to stay *after five o'clock* to finish all the work.
We went to a movie *after dinner*.
He had a hard time settling down to work *after his vacation*.
I have a doctor's appointment the day *after tomorrow*.

As a preposition of place, *after* means *behind* or *following behind*.

Be sure to close the door *after you*.
You'll have to get in line *after all these other people*; they were all here first.

After has several other meanings. It can be used to mean *following* and *as a result of*.

After the big mistake I made, they fired me.

After is also used in the sense of *in pursuit of*.

All the people were running *after the robber*.

It can also mean *concerning* or *about*.

Whenever I see her, she asks *after you*.

Another meaning of *after* is *in spite of*.

After all the work we did on the proposal, management still turned it down.

It is also used in the sense of *in the style of*, *in imitation of*.

His painting is not very original; you can see that it's all done *after Picasso*.

After can also mean *in honor of, with the name of*.

They named their daughter *after her grandmother*.
Washington, D.C., the capital of the United States, is named *after George Washington*, the nation's first president.

After can also mean *lower in rank than*.

I placed *after my friend* in the aptitude test.

against

Against as a place expression means *in contact with*.

He had his chair tilted back *against the wall*.
The book was resting *against the typewriter*.
I love the sound of rain beating *against the window*.

The other principal use of **against** is to express the idea of opposition.

Everyone is *against higher taxes*.
She always fought *against inequality*.

A similar meaning is *in contrast with*.

That painting looks nice *against the white wall*.

Against also means *in the opposite direction to*.

If you drive into town late in the afternoon, you'll be going *against the traffic*; everyone else will be coming out of town.

Against also indicates the idea of protection or defense.

The doctor vaccinated the baby *against polio*.
They're storing grain *against the possibility* of a bad harvest.

A further use of **against** is to indicate a commercial transaction on an account, or something received in exchange for something else.

I can't write a check *against my account* because I don't have enough money to cover it.

They can raise cash *against their accounts receivable.*

ahead of

Ahead of means *in advance of* or *in front of.*

There were several people standing *ahead of me* in the line.

We must check all of our information *ahead of the meeting.*

A lot of people will get *ahead of you* if you don't get a better education.

along

Along means *on a line the length of.*

There are a lot of stores *along the highway.*

I walked *along the road* to the town.

There are walls *along both sides of the field.*

alongside

Alongside means *at the side of, next to.*

We rode our bicycles *alongside the highway.*

There's a railroad line *alongside the factory.*

amid/amidst

Amid and **amidst** are literary prepositions that express the idea of *in the middle of* or *surrounded by.*

I couldn't see her *amid the dozens of people who thronged the room.*

She got lost *amidst all the confusion at the airport.*

among

Among is a more common preposition than **amid** or **amidst** to express the idea of *in the middle of* or *surrounded by.*

I saw her standing *among a large group of people.*

She finally found the letter *among all the other papers on her desk.*

Among expresses a choice or a division from an indefinite number of things.

You have to decide on five courses *among all those that the school offers.*
They've spread the work pretty evenly *among all the typists in the office.*

Among also expresses the idea of something done jointly or mutually.

They've reached an agreement *among themselves* to go on strike.
You shouldn't fight *among yourselves.*

Among is sometimes confused with **between**. **Among** is used with a large number or an indefinite number, whereas **between** is used with two things or people. Strict grammarians would confine the use of **between** to only two, but it is now widely used to refer to a small, limited number of things or people.

They'll have to make a choice for the promotion *among all the people in the office.*
They'll have to make a choice for the promotion *between him and me.*
They'll have to make a choice for the promotion *between Tom, Mary, and Stella.*
An agreement has been reached *among several nations* to launch a communications satellite.
An agreement has been reached *between France and England* to launch a communications satellite.
An agreement has been reached *between France, England, and Japan* to launch a communications satellite.

amongst

Amongst is the literary and poetic form of **among**.

apart from

Apart from is one of several expressions that indicate the idea of exception or exclusion.

> *Apart from the winter months*, it never rains here. (It only rains here in the winter months.)
> Her term paper was very good, *apart from a few spelling mistakes.*

around

Around, used both in expression of place and with verbs of motion, means *on all sides of, encircling, surrounding.*

> There's a fence *around the house.*
> We should go *around the city*, not through it.
> You'll have to walk *around the block* several times every day to get as much exercise as you need.

Around also means *here and there, at one place or another.*

> There were a lot of people standing *around the room.*
> There's a tool kit somewhere *around the house.*

A similar meaning of *around* is *in the area of.*

> She lives somewhere *around Eighth Street.*

Around can also be used in the sense of *on the basis of.*

> The society was built *around a belief in democracy.*

as

As is used as a preposition to mean *in the capacity of, with the function of.*

> She got a job *as a ticket agent with International Airlines.*
> He works *as a maintenance man* because he doesn't have any office skills.
> You shouldn't use that knife *as a screwdriver*; you'll break it.

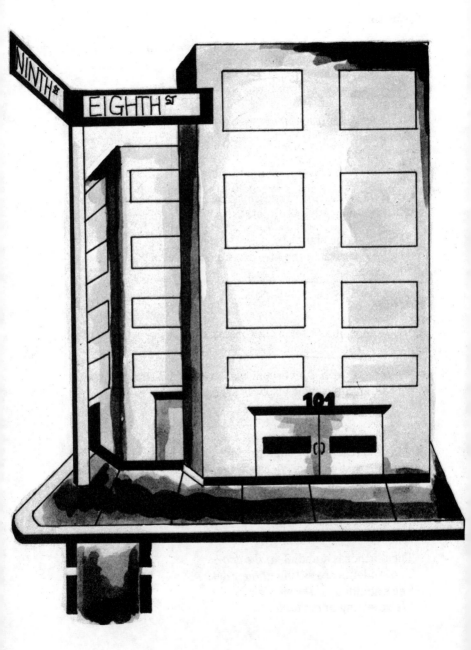

She lives somewhere *around Eighth Street*.

See *like* for the use of *as* as a conjunction and *like* as a preposition.

as for/as to

Both *as for* and *as to* mean *in reference to, concerning, regarding.*

> *As for the repairs to the roof,* we'll take care of them next month.
> *As to your proposal about the new budget procedures,* we'll discuss them at our next meeting.

as well as

As well as is another expression that indicates the idea of addition, one thing added to another.

> She's studying shorthand *as well as typing.*
> They're discussing the idea of using alcohol *as well as coal* to replace oil.

aside from

Aside from is one of several expressions that indicate the idea of exception or exclusion.

> *Aside from Janice,* everyone was present yesterday. (Janice was absent; everyone else was present.)

at

At is one of the most common of all prepositions. Indeed it is one of the most common words in the English language. *At* has a wide variety of uses in expression of place, time, and manner. In many of its uses, *at* can be confused with two other very common prepositions, *in* and *on*. *At*, in place expressions, means *near, almost touching.*

> The teacher is standing *at the door.*
> The students are sitting *at their desks.*
> She's standing *at the window.*
> We're sitting *at the table.*

At is used for specific places, often with a very strong sense of the purpose of being there.

We're sitting *at the table*. We're going to eat.
She's sitting *at her desk*. She's studying.
The men and women are *at work* now.
They ate *at a restaurant* last night.
I'm usually *at school* Monday and Wednesday afternoons.
He's *at the grocery store* now. He's buying food.

Either *in* or *at* can be used with *hospital*. *In* usually indicates that one is a patient, while *at* usually indicates a short visit.

He stayed *in the hospital* for several days after his operation.
The doctor's *at the hospital* now. She's examining her patients.

Similarly, *in school* refers to being a student for a period of time, while *at school* refers to being there at a particular time.

She's still *in school*. She has another year to go before she graduates.
You couldn't get me on the phone last night because I was *at school*.

In general, either *at* or *in* can be used for specific places that are enclosed. The choice between them usually depends on whether the idea of purpose is included or intended.

I saw them *at the store* while they were doing their weekly shopping.
I saw her *in the store*. I don't know why she was there.

At is used with a complete address, that is, one that includes the number of the house or building.

I live *at 695 West Tenth Street*.
Their house is *at 82 State Street*.
Her office is *at 918 Fifth Avenue*.

At is used in a number of common place expressions.

She's *at home* now.
They were *at dinner* when I called.

He's *at lunch* now.
I can't call you when I'm *at work*.

The sentences that follow illustrate the contrast between *in*, *on*, and *at* in place expressions.

They're studying *at a university in Tokyo*.
We stayed *at a hotel in New York*.
She's *at home* now. She's *in her room*.
I spent the afternoon *in my cabin on the ship*.
They live *in a house on a mountain*.
He was *at work in his office on the tenth floor*.

In time expressions, *at* is used with the hours of the day.

I got there *at exactly six forty-five*.
The meeting began *at nine o'clock*.
There's one flight *at four* and another *at five-thirty*.

At is also used in several other common time expressions.

She always goes out to lunch *at noon*.
I'm tired because I went to bed *at midnight* last night.
She didn't like working *at night*, so she got a daytime job.
We both arrived *at the same time*.

At can be used with the expressions *Easter* and *Christmas* when the context makes clear that the entire holiday season is meant. *On* is used for *Easter Sunday* or *Christmas Day* specifically.

We're going to go home *at Christmas* this year.
We always exchange presents *on Christmas Day*, never *on Christmas Eve*.

At is used in expressions of motion with the general sense of *toward* or *in the direction of*.

She was waving *at me*.
I'd jump *at the chance for a transfer*.

The following sentences illustrate the contrast between *in*, *on*, and *at* in time expressions.

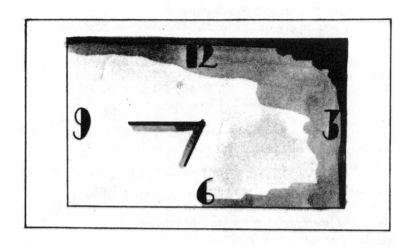

I got there *at exactly six forty-five.*

Our class begins *at ten o'clock in the morning*.
We're leaving *on the last Sunday in July*.
I'll meet you *at five o'clock in the afternoon on September 4th*.
We're giving a party *on Saturday at eight*.
I like to study *in the morning*, not *at night*.
We'll have a day off *on the first Monday in September*.
They were born *on the same day in 1960*.

At is also used in several expressions of manner, expressions that indicate the way in which something is done or that indicate a state or condition.

She's completely *at ease* with strangers.
The soldiers were standing *at attention*.
I'm not *at liberty* to give you that information.
He died last week; he's finally *at rest*.

We have seen that *at home* is a place expression, but it is also used as an expression of manner with a meaning similar to *at ease*.

It's taken her a few weeks to get used to her new duties, but now she's completely *at home* with them.

At is also used with an object towards which a thing or action is directed. With the verb *throw*, for example, *at* indicates an intention to strike or hit something or someone, whereas *to* indicates the intention for the object to be caught.

She threw the stone *at the dog* when it started to chase her.
I threw the ball *to him* and then he threw it back *to me*.
"It's time to go home now," she shouted *to the children*.
"Don't pull the dog's tail!" she shouted *at the children*.

At is used with actions and ideas that are the result of a feeling.

The baby smiled *at his mother*.
Everyone laughed *at her funny joke*.

Another use of *at* is with ages, speeds, levels, etc.

At 80 my grandmother still works in the garden every day.
He bought two dozen eggs *at $1.00* a dozen.

At is also used when a judgment is made.

> She's very good *at her job.*
> They're terrible *at planning parties.*

At can also mean *as a result of.*

> *At his suggestion,* we went to Puerto Rico for our vacation.

b

in back of

In back of is a place expression that indicates that one thing is behind or in the rear of another.

> There's a garage *in back of the house.*
> I sit *in back of her* in class.

In back of can also express the idea of support.

> I'm *in back of you* all the way in this matter. I'll support you to the very end.

because of

Because of is one of the expressions that is used for the idea of cause or reason.

> We were late *because of the traffic.*
> Communications were cut *because of the storm.*

before

In time expressions, *before* means *at an earlier time than.* In this sense, *before* is the opposite of *after.*

> I always do my homework just *before class.*
> I can't get there *before nine o'clock;* I just have too many other things to do.

In place expressions, *before* means *in front of, ahead of.*

There were so many people *before me* in line that I didn't get a chance for an interview for the job.

Before can also mean *in a higher or more important position.*

I always think of my family *before myself.*

In a similar sense, **before** means *ahead of in order or rank.*

There are only two people *before me* in my class; I got the third highest grade.

Before also means *in the presence of.*

Even though she's been on the stage for many years, she still gets nervous *before an audience.*

Before can also be used to express preference.

I'll always choose work *before play.*

in/on behalf of

In behalf of means *in the interest of* or *in support of.*

She spoke to us *in behalf of her favorite charity.*

On behalf of has the same meanings as *in behalf of*, but it has the additional meaning of *representing.*

I addressed the meeting *on behalf of my boss*, who couldn't be present herself.

behind

In expressions of place, *behind* has the same meaning as *in back of.*

There's a clock *behind my desk.*
They're planting a vegetable garden *behind their house.*

Another use of *behind* in place expressions is to indicate *on the other or on the farther side of.*

He was standing *behind the door* and listening to our conversation.

He was standing *behind the door* and listening to our conversation.

In time expressions, **behind** means *later than*.

The buses on that line always seem to run *behind schedule*.

Behind can also mean *inferior to, not up to the level of*.

He was *behind the other students* in math.

Behind is used to indicate support.

All the workers are *behind the union* in the strike.
She had some very important people *behind her*; that's why she got ahead so fast.

Behind often conveys the idea of something that is hidden or concealed.

I can't figure out what's *behind her remarks*. I don't know whether she's trying to help me or hurt me.
We're trying to discover what's going on *behind the scene*. Why is management keeping their decision a secret?

Behind also appears in a few common expressions.

I wish they'd stop talking *behind my back*. If they don't like my work, they should just tell me.
Our science textbook is way *behind the times*; it doesn't even mention the trip to the moon.

below

Below is used to indicate a lower level in place, rank, price, etc. In this sense **below** is the opposite of **above**.

There are several people *below Ms. Rivera* in the office; she has more authority than they do.
You'll be able to get a number of things *below the regular price* at the sale.
There's a small hotel just *below the top of the mountain*.
They're wearing their skirts *below the knee* this year.
The temperature has been *below zero* several days this winter.

Below also means *unworthy of*.

His suggestions have been so inadequate that they've really been *below our notice*.

beneath

Beneath has the same meanings as **below**, but in place expressions it often suggests that there is something hidden or something covering or overhanging the object of the preposition.

There's a coal mine *beneath this hill*.
The lake is *beneath a high hill*.
A corporal is *beneath a sergeant* in rank.

Beneath is more common than **below** to express the idea of unworthiness.

He felt that it was *beneath him* to ask for a promotion.

beside

Beside is used in place expressions with the meaning *by the side of, next to*.

There's a small table *beside my bed*.
She sits *beside me* in class.
There's a drugstore *beside the coffee shop*.

Beside can also be used to mean *compared with*.

Chemistry seemed easy to me *beside physics*.

A common expression is *beside the point*. It indicates something that is completely irrelevant or unrelated to the topic of the conversation, etc.

Everything he said was *beside the point*; it didn't have anything to do with what we were talking about.

Another expression is *beside oneself*, which means *out of one's senses because of strong emotion*.

She was *beside herself* with anxiety when her baby got sick.

besides

Besides is a very different word with very different meanings from **beside**. It is used most frequently to mean *in addition to*.

Besides physics, you'll have to study math.
I received one personal letter *besides all the usual ads* in the mail today.

Besides also means *other than*. In this sense, it is one of the prepositions that expresses the idea of exclusion.

Nobody in the office *besides Clara* is qualified to do that job.

between

Between means *in the space that separates two places, objects, times*, etc.

There's a laundry *between the drugstore and the post office*.
I'll meet you *between two and two-fifteen*.
There's a whole continent *between New York and San Francisco*.
The temperature this morning was somewhere *between fifty and sixty degrees Fahrenheit*.
That child is *between five and six years old*.
His job is *between clerical work and a junior management position*.

Between also has the idea of a shared activity of two or a limited number of persons.

We'll get the job done *between us*; you don't need to ask anyone else to help us.
Between you and me, I don't think he's doing a very good job.

Note that *me*, not *I*, follows **between**. The object forms of the personal pronouns always follow prepositions.

Between also expresses the idea of connection.

We have to strengthen the communications *between the different parts of the company*.

There's a laundry *between the drugstore and the post office*.

The marriage *between John Cooper and Sarah Brown* took place last Saturday.
Draw a line *between Point A and Point B.*

Between can also mean *involving.*

There's been a lot of controversy *between the members of the committee.*
We went to the basketball game *between the Lions and the Bears.*

Between is also used to express choice or division from two or a limited number of things or persons. For examples and for a discussion of the different uses of **between** and **among**, see **among**.

beyond

Beyond is used in place expressions to mean *on the far side of.*

The post office is just *beyond the barber shop.*
He's always wanted to find out what's *beyond those mountains.*

A similar meaning of **beyond** is *farther than.*

You have to go *beyond the railroad station* before you get to the hotel.
He can't see anything *beyond the job that he's working on at the moment.*

Beyond is occasionally used in time expressions to mean *later than.*

I don't have any plans *beyond next week.*
We stayed a day *beyond the date we'd intended to leave.*

Another meaning of **beyond** is *besides, except for.*

I don't know what to say *beyond "I'm sorry."*

Beyond is also used to indicate an idea that is outside or too much for comprehension, reach, etc.

It's *beyond my ability* to solve that problem.
Why she went out with him is *beyond me.*

Beyond is also used to mean *superior to.*

Her performance was *beyond any other that I've ever seen.*

In a similar meaning, **beyond** also expresses the idea of *more than, better than.*

The work she's done has been *beyond our expectations.*

A common expression is *beyond compare.* It means *very good.*

Her onion soup is *beyond compare.*

but

But is one of the most common words in English. Its most frequent use is as a conjunction that connects two independent clauses with contrasting ideas. **But** is also used as a preposition to express the idea of exclusion, that is, everybody or everything except the person, thing, or idea that follows the preposition.

Everyone *but me* had a hard time with the test.
No one could answer the question *but Marisa.*
We found everything *but the letter we were looking for.*

but for

But for is a phrase that expresses the idea of condition, like an *if*-clause. In the case of **but for**, the condition is negative. This is a rather literary expression rarely used in everyday speech.

But for her help, I couldn't have passed the exam. (If it hadn't been for her help, I couldn't have passed the exam.)
But for his lack of experience, he's well qualified for the job. (If it weren't for his lack of experience, he'd be well qualified for the job.)

by

By is a high-frequency preposition. One of its most common uses is to express the agent, the person, or thing that performs an action. In this sense, it is usually used with the passive voice.

These letters were written *by the boss.* (The boss wrote the letters.)
The checks are prepared *by computer.* (A computer prepares the checks.)

In a related meaning, **by** expresses the idea of instrument, the means or way by which an action is performed.

How are they going to ship their household goods?
They're going to ship them *by air.*
How did you travel around Japan?
We traveled *by train* most of the time.
What's the most expensive way to ship books?
The most expensive way is *by air.*
What's the cheapest way?
The cheapest is usually *by water.*

In place expressions, **by** has the idea of *near* or *next to.*

There's a lamp *by my bed.*
He always sits *by the door* so that he can be the first person to leave the room.

With verbs of motion, **by** has the meaning of *past, without stopping.*

She walked *by me* without even saying hello.
The bus went right *by the corner where I wanted to get off.* (The bus didn't stop.)
We drove *by New York,* but we didn't go into the city itself.

By is used in time expressions with the idea of *not later than.*

I have to get to the office *by nine o'clock.*
The plane should arrive *by noon.*
They have to reach an agreement with the union *by midnight tonight*; otherwise, the workers will go out on strike.
We'll be in Paris *by this time tomorrow.*

By can express the idea of doing something in a fixed period of time.

She works *by the day.* (Her wages are figured on a daily basis.)
We get paid *by the week.*

I have to get to the office *by nine o'clock*.

By can also mean *during*, that is, *through a period of time* or *at some point in a period of time*.

He made the trip *by night* because he wanted to take care of his business the next morning.

Still another meaning of *by* is *following*.

You can't just go ahead day *by day*; you have to have a plan of some kind.
He talked to us one *by one*, not all together in a group.

By is used to give the reason for a judgment.

I can tell *by your face* that you are surprised.

By is used in giving measurements and in formulas for multiplication.

My room is *12 feet by 10*.
Tomatoes are sold *by the pound*.
The picture I want to get framed is *20 inches by 16*.
When you multiply *4 by 5*, you get 20.

Another use of *by* is to show an amount or a degree.

His horse won the race *by a nose*.
Silver is more expensive *by far* than tin.

By is also used in the same sense as *in behalf of*.

The company has done very well *by its employees*; they all benefit from the profit-sharing plan.

A common expression with *by* is *by oneself*, meaning *alone without help*.

The child can't get dressed *by himself*. His parents have to help him.

c

in case of

In case of is a phrase that is used as a preposition with a conditional meaning like an *if*-clause. *In case of* has an affirmative significance.

In case of fire, you should use the stairway. (If there's a fire, you should use the stairway.)

circa

Circa is a Latin preposition which has been taken into English to indicate an approximate date. It is often abbreviated *c.* when it appears in encyclopedias or other reference materials.

Columbus, Christopher (*c. 1466-1506*). That is, Columbus was born *circa 1466*; the approximate date of his birth was 1466—the exact date is unknown.

Circa is considered a foreign word in English and therefore is usually written in italic letters, like most other foreign expressions.

close to

Close to is a phrase that expresses the idea of nearness or proximity either in place or time.

My house is *close to the railroad station*.
The factory is located *close to a highway*.
They're *close to a solution*, but they haven't quite reached it yet.
We'll be there *close to four o'clock*.
The baby is *close to two years old*.

concerning

Concerning is a present participle that is used as a preposition meaning *relating to, in regard to, about*. It often appears in business or government correspondence or other rather formal usage.

I am writing to you *concerning the invoice that I received from you.*
They're going to have a meeting *concerning the budget.*

considering

Considering is another present participle which can be used as a preposition. It means *in view of* or *taking into account.*

Considering his size, he's very strong. (He isn't very tall.)
The work was done very quickly and efficiently *considering all the problems we encountered.*

contrary to

Contrary to means *opposite to* or *altogether different from.*

Contrary to the widespread rumors, our company is not in financial difficulty.
Contrary to his expectations, he was never altogether successful. (He expected to be a big success.)

d

despite

Despite is one of a group of prepositions that are similar in meaning to sentence connectors like **but**, which expresses the idea of contrast or opposition. A sentence with **despite** means that something is true or possible even though the prepositional phrase with **despite** is in opposition or contrast to the rest of the sentence. **Despite** is a somewhat formal and literary expression.

He has continued to work *despite his illness.*
They are going ahead with their plan to build the dam *despite protests* from the people who will have to move.

down

Down is used more often as an adverb than as a preposition. As a preposition, it occurs with verbs of motion to mean *from* *a higher to a lower level.* In this sense, **down** is the opposite of **up**.

> He hurt himself when he fell *down the stairs.*
> The children ran *down the mountain.*
> The stone rolled *down the hill.*

Both **down** and **up** are frequently used in expressions such as *down the street, up the street,* etc. In some cases, this may indicate an actual change in level from higher to lower with **down** or from lower to higher with **up**. In other cases, it may mean from a higher- to a lower-numbered street with **down** (you go **down** to 14th Street from 42nd Street) or from a lower- to a higher-numbered street with **up**. Often it simply depends on the numbering of the buildings on the street, on local usage, or on the speaker's own perception of what constitutes **down** or **up**.

due to

Due to is used as a preposition meaning *caused by.*

> The accident was *due to his carelessness.*

Due to is also used colloquially in the same sense as **because of**.

> We were late *due to the storm.*

The use of **due to** with verbs is criticized by traditional grammarians, but is nevertheless widespread.

during

During is a preposition that indicates the entire length of time of an action. It is often preceded by *all* in this sense.

> There have been many advances in technology *during my lifetime.*
> It rained *all during the night.*
> She's made steady progress *all during the year.*

During is also used to mean *at one time or another within a period of time.*

I'll be in the office *during the afternoon*, but I don't know exactly when; it may be around two or three o'clock.

I was in the city *during July*, but I can't remember whether it was the second or third week of the month.

e

except

Except is one of the prepositions like **but** that excludes the object of the preposition from the action of the rest of the sentence.

All the children *except Phil* were playing outdoors.
She's done well in all her courses *except history*.
I've finished all my work *except this one letter*.

Except is sometimes followed by **for**, especially at the beginning of the sentence.

Except for history, she's done well in all her courses.
Except for February, this has been an unusually dry year.

f

in favor of

The phrase *in favor of* expresses the idea of support or approval.

Everybody is *in favor of cutting taxes*.
I'm not *in favor of either of the candidates*.

In a similar sense, *in favor of* indicates a choice or preference.

I turned down a job in Dallas *in favor of a better one in Seattle*.

for

For is one of the prepositions with a high degree of frequency.

All the children *except Phil* were playing outdoors.

It is used in a large number of adverbial phrases, many of which express the idea of purpose.

He went to the store to get some bread.
He went to the store *for bread.*
She's returning to school to get her master's degree.
She's returning to school *for her master's degree.*
They're going to a restaurant to have lunch.
They're going to a restaurant *for lunch.*
I took this job to get some experience.
I took this job *for the experience.*

A related meaning expresses the idea of suitability.

It's a cool night; it'll be a good night *for sleeping.*
I've found a good spot *for watching the parade.*

For is also used with verbs of motion to indicate destination. In this case, it means *with the purpose of reaching* the destination.

He started *for the bank*, but he never got there.
She left *for home* about an hour ago.

For is also used to mean *in/on behalf of* or *for the benefit of.*

She wants me to do some errands *for her.*
I'm going to give a speech *for the candidate.*
He always has his lawyer act *for him* in his business affairs.
She takes care of all public relations *for the company.*
Ms. Conklin handles the accounts receivable *for us.*

For is also used to mean *in place of, instead of, as a substitute for.*

I made the mistake, but she took the blame *for me.*
Ted's sick today, so Jim's filling in *for him.*
They make a lot of things nowadays where plastic is substituted *for metal or wood.*
You can use margarine *for butter* in this recipe.

For is also used to mean *in honor of* or *honoring.*

She gave a birthday party *for her daughter.*
We attended the banquet they gave *for the mayor* last night.

He went to the store *for bread*.

For also means *considering the nature of.*

> It's terribly hot *for this time of year.*
> It still isn't very cold *for January.*

A related meaning is *in proportion to.*

> He's very tall *for his age.*
> She's too intelligent *for the work she's doing.*

Still another meaning of **for** is *in favor of, in support of.*

> Of course all the candidates are *for lower taxes;* in an election year, nobody is *for higher taxes.*
> I don't want to vote *for any of the candidates* in the next election.

When **for** is followed by *all*, it often has a meaning similar to **despite**.

> He couldn't solve this problem *for all the math he's studied.*
> *For all her experience*, she can't get a good job. (Even though she's had a lot of experience, she can't get a good job.)

Another meaning of **for** followed by *all* is *considering how little.*

> *For all I know*, she may be arriving tonight. (I don't know when she'll be arriving.)

For is also used with sums of money to mean *to the amount of* or *at a price of.*

> The plumber sent me a bill *for fifty dollars.*
> She received a check *for several hundred dollars.*
> Oranges are six *for a dollar* this week.
> They have shirts on sale. They're selling them at two *for fifteen dollars.*

For is used to indicate the person or thing toward which an action is directed for some purpose.

> The office manager sent *for me;* she wanted to talk to me about my work.

We sent *for sandwiches and coffee* because we didn't have time to go out *for lunch*.
This recipe calls *for a pound of tomatoes*.
I didn't have anything to write with, so I had to ask *for a pen*.

For and **of** are both used after *good* and *bad*, but with different meanings. *Good for* or *bad for* indicates that the action named will have a good or bad effect on the object of *for*. *Good of* or *bad of* indicates that it is good or bad that the object of *of* has performed the action; in other words, the person speaking likes or doesn't like the action.

It will be good *for you* to get more exercise; it will make you healthier.
Smoking so much is bad *for you*; it will harm your health.
It was good *of you* to remember to bring this book. I've been looking forward to reading it.
It was bad *of her* to write that letter; it caused a lot of trouble.

For, like **to**, can be used with a noun or object pronoun as a substitute for an indirect object, especially after *buy*, *get*, *make*, and *sing*.

She bought her children a book.
She bought a book *for her children*.
She bought it *for them*.
I got him a pencil.
I got a pencil *for him*.
I got it *for him*.
I made this scarf *for you*.
He's going to sing a song *for us*.

For has another important functional use. It is used before a noun or pronoun which indicates the subject of an infinitive following several adjectives in sentences beginning with *It is*, etc.

It's important to get regular exercise.
It's important *for you* to get regular exercise.
It was hard to understand the problem.
It was hard *for me* to understand the problem.

It's necessary to get some experience.
It's necessary *for her* to get some experience.
It will be easy to call me.
It will be easy *for you* to call me.

For is also used in expressions of time. *For* indicates the duration of the action, that is, the length of time that the action lasted.

She lived in New York *for two years.*
He's only worked here *for a few months.*
I have to talk to you *for a minute or two.*
I'll be away *for the weekend.*

For is used in time expressions to indicate a single action, whereas *during* is used to express one that is habitual or occurs over a period of time.

She has a temporary job *for today*, but she doesn't have one *for tomorrow.*
She has one job *during the day* and another *during the evening.*
She's been holding down both jobs *for quite a long time now.*

For is also contrasted with *since* in time expressions. *For*, as we have seen, covers a period of time, whereas *since* indicates the point of time at which the action began. *Since* is used with present perfect or past perfect verb phrases.

She's worked here *for two months.*
She's worked here *since October.*
He's been on vacation *for a few days.*
He's been on vacation *since Thursday.*
I haven't seen them *for several years.*
I haven't seen them *since 1978.*
I'd been waiting to see him *for an hour.*
I'd been waiting to see him *since ten o'clock.*

from

From in place expressions and with verbs of motion indicates the point of origin or the source of the action.

The children walk home *from school* every afternoon.

The children walk home *from school* every afternoon.

She comes *from Brazil.*
She got her coat *from a store in the suburbs.*
You can't remove reference books *from the library.*
There's a wonderful view *from the top of this building.*
I received some good news *from my friend.*
I got the information *from our computer.*

From can often be replaced by **out of** in describing motion.

I want to take these books *from the library.*
I want to take these books *out of the library.*
He ran *from the house.*
He ran *out of the house.*
She pulled her keys *from her pocketbook.*
She pulled her keys *out of her pocketbook.*

Sometimes **out of** indicates only *from the inside to the outside*, whereas **from** indicates only origin or source.

I moved the old sofa *out of the house* to make room for the new one.
They moved *from Chicago* last year.

From also has the sense of *in the opposite direction to. Away* is often used before **from** to emphasize this meaning.

He was running *from the police.*
You can't escape *from your responsibilities.*
I want to find a place to work *away from all this noise.*
The burglar ran *away from the house.*

From is also used for the idea of distance, especially in the expressions *a long way from* and *far from. A long way from* is used in affirmative statements and *far from* is used in negative statements. Either can be used in questions.

My house is only twenty miles *from my office.*
The library is *a long way from here.*
The school isn't *far from my apartment.*
Is the hotel *a long way from the center of town?*
Is the theater *far from our hotel?*

From is often used to show the time when an action begins when **to** is used to show the time when the action ends.

We work *from nine to five* every day.
The class lasts *from six to seven fifteen* every evening.
I lived in San Francisco *from 1980 to 1982*.

From can also be used alone to show the beginning time of the action when the phrase is modified.

You have to start doing your work carefully *from this moment on*.
She showed how bright she was *from the day she was born*.
He didn't get along with anyone in the office *from the minute he walked in the door*.

From is used to indicate the process of subtraction.

Three from five leaves two.
Seven from eight is one.
Six from nine equals three.

in front of

In front of is the opposite of **in back of**. **In front of** has the same meaning in place expressions as **ahead of** or **before**.

She usually parks *in front of the house*, even though there's a garage in back of it.
There were two people *in front of me* in line and three others in back of me.

In front of does NOT mean *across from* or *opposite*.

The post office is *across from the hotel*.
There's a mailbox *in front of the post office*.

i

in

In is a high-frequency preposition with many different meanings. In place expressions, **in** means *inside, within some kind of definite limits*.

This is my room. There's a bed *in the room*. There's a chair *in the room*, too. I also have a table lamp *in my room*.
I always keep everything *in the same place in my desk*.
I keep stamps *in the top drawer*.
I keep pens and pencils *in the top drawer*, too.
There are also some paperclips *in the top drawer*.
I keep paper and envelopes *in the middle drawer*.
I keep files *in the bottom drawer*.

In is used with the names of continents, countries, states, provinces, or cities. It is also used with the names of mountain ranges.

They live *in Montreal*.
Montreal is *in Quebec*.
Quebec is a province *in Canada*.
She went to visit friends *in Belo Horizonte*.
Belo Horizonte is *in Brazil*.
Brazil is *in South America*.
I have some friends *in San Francisco*.
San Francisco is *in California*.
California is *in the United States*.
Quito is located *in the Andes*.
There are a lot of ski resorts *in the Adirondacks*.

There are several common place expressions with *in*.

I was *in bed* when you called.
She's *in conference* now.
They live *in the country*, not *in the city*.
Did you leave your key *in the car*?
There are two passengers *in the taxi*.
They like to go camping *in the mountains*.

In time expressions, *in* is used with centuries, years, seasons, and months.

Who knows what will happen *in the twenty-first century*?
The Industrial Revolution began *in the eighteenth century*.
She was born *in 1960*.
I started working for this company *in 1981*.
They always take their vacation *in the summer*.
It gets very cold here *in the winter*.
School will start *in September*, and it will end *in June*.

This is my room. There's a bed *in the room*. There's a chair *in the room*, too. I also have a table lamp *in my room*.

There are several common time expressions with *in*.

I always get up early *in the morning*.
She takes care of her correspondence *in the evening*.
I don't often go out *in the evening*.

See *at* for examples of the different uses of *in*, *on*, and *at* in place and time expressions.

In is used with verbs of motion or direction with the idea of entering or putting something in an enclosed space or area.

She's coming *in the door* right now.
You can put all those papers *in this box*.
When I finish the letters, I put them *in my out-box*.
I saw her go *in the conference room*.

In is also used in several expressions of manner, those that indicate the way in which something is done or that indicate a state or condition.

They didn't have any money, so they paid him *in kind*; they gave him the food that they had grown on their farms.
Your remarks are not *in order*; you should wait to be recognized by the chairperson before you speak.
He keeps up with everything new; his clothes are always *in fashion*.
That factory hasn't been *in use* for several years.
We have the report *in hand* now; we should be able to make a decision soon.
Her behavior was not *in line* with company policy.

inside

Inside has the same general meaning as *in*, that is, *within limits in time or place*. *Inside* is usually somewhat more emphatic than *in*.

My cat likes to stay *inside the house* all the time.
There are too many people *inside the museum*. Let's stay out here for a while.
I'll finish the letter *inside an hour*.

48

Inside often conveys the idea of something concealed, hidden, lost, mislaid, etc.

> I found some old letters *inside the trunk.*
> There was a key *inside the box.*

In colloquial use, **inside** is sometimes followed by *of.*

> There were four people *inside of the room.*
> I'll finish it *inside of an hour.*

instead of

Instead of means *in place of* or *as a substitute for.*

> They've chosen her *instead of me* for a promotion.
> They sent us a carbon copy of the letter *instead of the original.*
> You can use margarine *instead of butter* in this recipe.
> Aluminum is often used *instead of steel* in modern construction.

into

Into has the same general meaning as *in* in expressions of motion or direction, but **into** makes the meaning more exact than *in*. For example, *She's walking in the room* can mean either that she's entering the room or that she's walking around inside the room. Therefore, **into** should be used whenever there's any possibility of misunderstanding.

> She's walking *into the room* now.
> You can put all those papers *into this box.*
> I saw her go *into the conference room*, but she hasn't come out yet.
> The thief broke *into the store* and stole a thousand dollars.

In a similar sense, **into** can mean *colliding with.*

> The car went out of control and ran *into a tree.*

Into is occasionally used with expressions of time to mean *entering that period of time.*

They had so much to say to each other that they talked long *into the night*.

Into is also used to express the idea of division.

They're going to break up the company *into several different sections*.
She cut the cake *into eight pieces*.
Five *into ten* is two.

Into is also used in several expressions to indicate a state or condition.

They've gone *into business* for themselves.
She kissed the prince and he turned *into a frog*.
You'll have to translate this letter *into English* so we can understand it.

l

less

Less is used as a preposition to indicate subtraction.

Seven less five is two.
The net profit is the gross income *less expenses and taxes*.

like

The preposition ***like*** means *similar to*, *resembling*, or *characteristic of*.

She has a memory *like a computer*.
It isn't *like you* to make so many mistakes.
He looks *like his father*.
This rabbit tastes just *like chicken*.

Like can also express the idea of wanting or desiring.

I feel *like eating out* tonight; I'm tired of my own cooking.

The use of ***like*** as a conjunction instead of ***as*** or ***as if*** has been increasing, even though it is still considered non-standard by traditional grammarians. Many people say "It looks *like* it's going to snow" instead of "It looks *as if* it's going to snow"; or "You have to do this just *like* the directions say" instead of "You have to do this just *as* the directions say." It is preferable to use *like* only as a preposition.

m

minus

Minus is a Latin word that has been taken into English as a preposition to express the idea of subtraction.

Eight minus four equals four.
You have a balance of 87 dollars in your account *minus the check that you wrote on the account* today.

n

near

Near is a preposition of high frequency which expresses the idea of proximity, that is, a close relationship in space, time, degree, etc.

My apartment is *near the office*; it only takes me about ten minutes to get to work.
Philadelphia is *near New York*. The two cities are only about 90 miles apart.
I'm going to take a vacation *near the end of the year*.
She always adds up the day's receipts *near closing time*.
The temperature was *near zero* when I got up this morning.
They're *near an agreement* on a new contract.

next to

Next to is a preposition of place that means *immediately at the side of, in the nearest position to.*

There's a wastebasket *next to my desk*.

I sit *next to Alice* in math class.
The hardware store is right *next to the drugstore*.
There's a garage *next to our building*.

Next to is occasionally used to express the idea of closest in rank or order.

I'm *next to Helen* in math. She got 92 on the exam, and I got 91.
Next to French cooking, I like northern Italian best.

notwithstanding

Notwithstanding is a preposition that expresses the same idea as *despite*, that is, it introduces something that is in opposition or contrast to the rest of the sentence.

They went ahead with their plans for the picnic *notwithstanding the prediction of rain*.
They managed to stay in business *notwithstanding their cash flow problems*.

Like *despite*, **notwithstanding** is rather formal. The most commonly used expression in this group of prepositions is the phrase *in spite of*.

O

of

Of is one of the most common words in English, and like most other high-frequency words, it has several different meanings. One of them is to introduce adjective phrases with the general meaning of *belonging to* or *pertaining to*.

All the records *of the company* were destroyed in the fire.
The officers *of the club* are elected every January.
I had to see the manager *of the store* to get a refund.
The interview with the mayor *of the city* will be shown on TV this evening.

English has an inflected possessive form, -'s with singular nouns and irregular plurals and -s' with regular plurals. For this reason, *of* is seldom used to indicate possession, especially when talking about people.

I want you to read Janet's letter.
I walked over to my friend's apartment.
You haven't seen the children's room, have you?
They asked me to wait in the teachers' lounge.
She showed me her parents' house.

Of, however, does introduce phrases of possession with *own*.

She's started a business *of her own*.
The children have a room *of their own*.
He doesn't want to share an apartment. He wants a place *of his own*.

On can also introduce phrases with *own* when they are used in the sense of *without help*. These phrases are adverbial rather than adjectival.

He did all the work *on his own*; nobody gave him a hand.
You have to answer this letter *on your own*; I'm not going to tell you what to say.

Of can also mean *belonging to* in the sense of *being a part of*.

The door *of the car* was stuck.
The deck *of the ship* was swept by a huge wave.
One leg *of this table* has been broken.
The cover *of a book* doesn't usually tell much about what's inside.
We've just painted the side *of the house*.
I've worn out the collar *of this shirt*.

One of the most common meanings of *of* is *pertaining to*.

He's sent us a transcript *of his academic record*.
The patterns *of English grammar* are easy to learn.
The bank will send you a statement *of your account* every month.
We have complete records *of all our sales*.
You should prepare a résumé *of your previous experience*.
We can't locate any record *of that transaction*.

53

Another frequent meaning of *of* is *characteristic of.*

> The color *of oxygen* is blue.
> Our professor is a woman *of great learning.*
> I don't worry about the style *of my clothes.*
> The quality *of their products* is always high.
> The strength *of steel* has made it an important material in modern industry.
> I don't like the taste *of turnips.*

Of is frequently used in the related meanings of *made of* or *consisting of.*

> They put up a wall *of red brick* all around their property.
> We passed field after field *of wheat.*
> This rug is made *of cotton and wool.*
> We had a quick lunch *of bread and cheese.*

The prepositional phrase with *of* can often be replaced by a noun adjunct—a noun used as an adjective—in the sense of *made of* or *consisting of.*

> They put up a red brick wall all around their property.
> We passed one wheat field after another.
> I use aluminum pots and pans for cooking, but I really prefer ceramic.
> There's a vegetable garden in back of their house.

Of is also used to indicate the source or origin of the noun that is modified by the prepositional phrase. In this case, it is often followed by a proper noun, the name of a person or place.

> I've read all the novels *of Ernest Hemingway.*
> She especially likes the symphonies *of Mozart.*
> The wines *of California* have improved in quality in recent years.
> The voters *of the United States* choose a president every four years.

Of is used in the sense of containing.

> I left a pack *of cigarettes* in the car.
> I had to pay twenty dollars for one small bag *of groceries!*

Of is also used after ordinal numbers (*first, second, third*, etc.) or other words that express order in giving times and dates.

> Monday is the first day *of the work week* for most people.
> This is the last day *of the pay period.*
> The French national holiday is the 14th *of July.*
> I'll begin my vacation on the 10th *of October.*
> I have to walk home at the darkest hour *of the night.*

Of is used in expressions of distance after words like *east, west*, etc.

> Chicago is west *of New York.*
> The factory is only a few miles south *of the city.*

Of often occurs as part of phrases like *a piece of* that are used when it is necessary to express the idea of number in connection with a mass noun (a noun that cannot be counted).

> I don't want two pieces *of bread*; one will be plenty.
> There's a big pile *of correspondence* in my in-basket.
> The wind blew a grain *of sand* into her eye.
> I felt a drop *of rain* a few minutes ago.
> The cowboys drove the herd *of cattle* to the railhead.

In general, an adjective phrase with **of** makes the meaning of the noun it modifies more specific. These phrases often answer the questions *Which?*, *What?*, or *What kind of?*

> Have you seen the pictures?
> Which pictures?
> The pictures *of my family.*
> We'll soon come to the end.
> The end *of what?*
> The end *of the school year.*
> We're going to a concert tonight.
> What kind *of concert?*
> A concert *of classical music.*

Of has a very important use in forming partitive phrases, phrases that indicate part of a whole. They can be formed with any word that expresses number or quantity, including adjectives in the comparative and the superlative.

There's some information missing.
Some *of the information* is missing.
Many people in this area are not going to vote in the election.
Many *of the people* in this area are not going to vote in the election.
He wants to see all *of us*.
Some *of you* have to study quite a lot harder.
I don't know where the rest *of my friends* have gone.
I've read part *of this report*, but I haven't read all *of it* yet.
Jim is the taller *of the two players*.
She's the best *of the new employees*.

Of is also used in a few adverbial phrases. One of these expresses the idea of being separated from something.

He was held up last night and robbed *of his watch and wallet*.
She feels she's been cheated *of a promotion*.
I've been relieved *of my duties*.

Of can also be used to indicate result.

Nobody has died *of smallpox* in recent years.

off

Off is most frequently used as a preposition of place with several related meanings. In one sense, it means *away from* or *no longer in contact with*.

She knocked the cup *off the table*.
She was hurt when she fell *off her bike*.
He drove his car *off the road*.
I took the phone *off the hook* so I could get some sleep.

Off is also used in the sense of *branching away from* or *leading away from*.

Her house is on a little road just *off the highway*.

Off can also mean *at a distance from*.

The ship was only a mile *off the coast* when it sank.
Their house is only a few yards *off the main highway*.

She knocked the cup *off the table*.

Off also means *away from* in the sense of *being no longer on duty*.

I get *off work* at five o'clock, so I can meet you downtown at around six.

She's *off duty* on Monday, so she takes care of all her housework then.

Off is used in expressions of manner to indicate the idea of *living from the substance of*.

They live *off the land*; everything they eat and wear comes from their farm.

Off also means *not at the usual level or standard*.

He wanted to run the mile faster than it had ever been done, but he was *off the record* by more than a second.

In a colloquial use, *off* means *abstaining from*.

I want to lose weight, so I'm *off sweets* for a while.

Another informal use of *off* is in the expression *off the record* which means *unofficially* or *in private*.

Our interview was *off the record*; the reporter shouldn't have included that information in her article.

Note the number of negative uses of *off*. In many senses, it serves as the opposite of *on*.

on

On is another of the high-frequency prepositions with many different meanings. In place expressions, *on* indicates *on top of*, *on the surface of*, *in contact with*, or *touching the surface of*.

This is my room. I'm sitting *on the bed*. There are two pictures *on the wall*. There's a lamp *on the table*.

There are a lot of letters *on my desk*. There's a lamp *on my desk*. There's a telephone *on my desk*, too. There's also a typewriter *on my desk*. My coat is hanging *on the chair*. I left my hat *on the chair*, too.

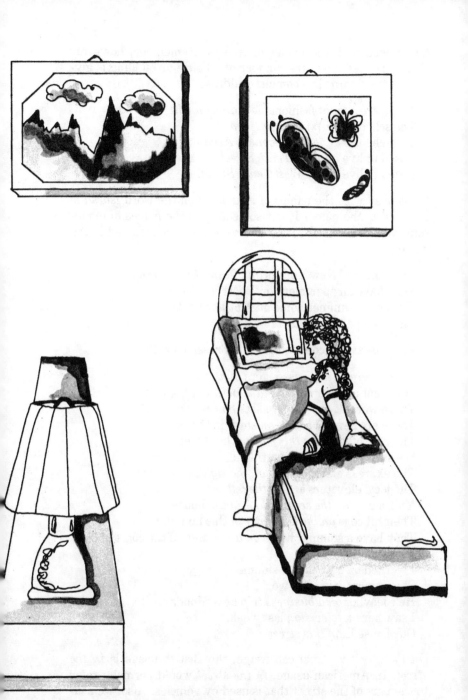

This is my room. I'm sitting *on the bed*. There are two pictures *on the wall*. There's a lamp *on the table*.

On is used with the names of streets. Remember, however, that *at* is used when the number of a house or building is given, in other words in a complete address.

There are a lot of fashionable stores *on Fifth Avenue.*
The school is *on Wisconsin Avenue.*
The school is *at 5634 Wisconsin Avenue.*
I used to live *on West Tenth Street.*
I used to live *at 689 West Tenth Street.*

On is used with the names of islands when the word *island* is included in the name. It is also used with the names of mountains when the words *mount* or *mountain* are included in the name.

The center of New York is *on Manhattan Island.*
They have an apartment *on Roosevelt Island.*
We have a summer home *on Mount Shasta.*
There's a park *on Bear Mountain.*

There are several common place expressions with *on.*

There weren't any passengers *on the bus.*
We spent an hour *on the plane* before it took off.
There weren't any empty seats *on the train.*
There are several actors *on stage* in that scene.
The post office is *on this side* of the street.
We stayed *on the ship* overnight.
The express elevators are *on the right.*
The local elevators are *on the left.*
My room is *on the second floor* of the house.
Their office is *on the 20th floor* of this building.
They have a summer home *on an island* off the coast of New England.
I worked *on a farm* last summer.
She's *on vacation* this week.
He's leaving *on a business trip* next Monday.
I saw her *on television* last week.
Our house is *on this street.*

On the street is American usage; the British usage is *in the street.* In American usage, *in the street* would normally refer to the part of the street that is used by vehicles. Also, we usually sit *on* an armless chair, but *in* an armchair. We also sit *on* a sofa or *on* a couch. See *at* for examples of the uses of *in*, *on*, and *at* in place expressions.

In time expressions, *on* is used with the days of the week, the days of the month, and with the names of holidays.

> I have an appointment with her *on Tuesday.*
> The convention will begin *on the 18th of June.*
> My birthday falls *on Monday* this year.
> We're going to have our exam *on the 6th.*
> They're moving *on March 12th.*
> Many families get together for a big dinner *on Thanksgiving.*

On is used with time words like *night, evening, afternoon,* etc., when the indefinite article *a* or *an* or some other indefinite expression comes before the time word.

> It happened *on a night* in November, but I can't remember the exact date.
> We'll have our meeting *on a morning* next week, but I'm not yet sure which one.

On is used with time words that are followed by an adjective clause or a prepositional phrase.

> The car broke down *on the day that they were supposed to leave on their vacation.*
> I got sick *on the morning of the exam.*

There are a few other common time expressions with *on*.

> I met them *on holiday.*
> He tries to get some exercise *on his day off.*
> We always do our shopping *on the same day.*
> The plane arrived *on time*; it wasn't early and it wasn't late.

See *at* for examples of the uses of *in*, *on*, and *at* in time expressions. *On* is used with verbs of motion to mean *going* or *entering on the surface* or *on top of something.* The phrase with *on* is often preceded by *out*.

> There was a loud cheer when he walked *out on the platform.*
> The audience applauded when she stepped *on the stage.*

On is occasionally used to express the same meaning as **about** or **concerning**, that is, *on the subject of*.

The workers will vote *on a strike* tomorrow.
They expect to make an announcement *on the sale of the company* next week.
They can't agree *on anything*.

On can also mean *partaking of*.

They've had the patient *on antibiotics* for several days.

On is used in a number of common expressions of manner; occasionally they're in a sort of borderline area between time, place, and manner.

All the passengers are *on board* now, so we can leave.
The doctor is always *on call*. She has to leave a telephone number with the hospital switchboard no matter where she goes so they can get in touch with her in case of an emergency.
I go *on duty* at noon, and I get off duty at eight in the evening.
We have a good deal of information *on file*.
Help! Help! The house is *on fire*!
We had to cover the last few miles *on foot* because there was no road.
He's always *on guard*; he's always careful about what he says.
We have plenty of envelopes *on hand*; we don't need to order any more.
The peanuts are *on the house*; you don't have to pay for them.
They're going to bring the new generator *on line* this week. It should be in operation by Tuesday.
We have the machine parts *on order*; they should be delivered sometime next week.
It wasn't an accident; he did it *on purpose*.
I'm saying this *on the record*; you can quote my words exactly.
The workers are *on strike*. They'll stay out until management agrees to pay them more.
Because of the computer, we have a great deal of informa-

tion *on tap*. The information is available to us at a moment's notice.

Note also this special use of the phrase *on time*.

They bought their new refrigerator *on time*. They'll pay for it in regular monthly installments.

onto

Onto gives a more exact meaning than *on* with verbs of motion.

There was a loud cheer when he walked *onto the platform*.
My room opens *onto a large balcony*.
We have to drive about five miles before we turn *onto the highway*.

opposite

Opposite means *facing* or *across from*.

My house is *opposite a big park*.
There are several good restaurants *opposite the hotel*.

out/out of

Out is almost always used as an adverb rather than a preposition. As a preposition it is often combined with *of* to mean *from the interior to the exterior*.

I was looking *out the window* when I saw her.
She just walked *out the door*.
She was walking *out of the room* when I called her.
I took some pencils *out of the box*.

Out of is also used in the sense of *absent from*.

He's going to be *out of town* all week.
She'll be *out of the office* this afternoon.
The children were *out of school* for two days.

Another meaning of *out of* is *having used the entire supply of*.

We're *out of paper* for the photocopier; we'll have to order more right away.

She's just gone to the store; she was *out of bread and milk.*

A similar meaning is *no longer working* or *no longer in a working condition.*

He's been *out of work* for two months, but he expects to get a job soon.

The elevator is *out of service* today; it's being repaired.

A similar meaning is *no longer in a particular state or condition.*

The plane went *out of control* and crashed to the ground.

That expression is *out of fashion*; no one uses it anymore.

She woke up *out of a sound sleep* when the phone rang.

Out of is also used to mean *from the number of.*

Ten *out of the twenty applicants for the job* are not qualified.

They chose me *out of all the people in the office* to go into the management training program.

Out of is used with verbs like *make, form, shape*, etc., to indicate a material.

Many modern buildings are made *out of steel and glass.*

The statue was shaped *out of a single piece of marble.*

Out of is occasionally used to mean *by reason of* or *because of.*

You should ask what to do; it isn't necessary to make mistakes *out of ignorance.*

Another meaning of *out of* is *beyond.*

She was already *out of sight* when I remembered what I wanted to tell her.

Out of can also express the idea of depriving someone of something.

They've cheated me *out of a promotion.*

Out of also appears in a few familiar expressions.

Don't pay any attention to her; she's *out of her mind.* (She's crazy.)

They were *out of their minds with grief* when their only son died.

My boss turned down my request for a raise; she said it was *out of the question,* just impossible.

outside

Outside means *on the exterior* or *beyond the limits of.*

I want to see him *outside the office* someday.

When the dog gets *outside the fence,* he tries to chase cars.

In colloquial use, **outside** is sometimes followed by **of,** but this is considered non-standard. However, **outside of** is sometimes used to express the idea of exclusion.

Outside of Thursday, I won't be free any day this week.

Outside of one day last week, we haven't had any rain for a month.

over

Over is used both as an adverb and a preposition. As a preposition, it has several different meanings. Its most frequent use is *at or to a higher level in place, authority, degree,* etc.

There are a lot of clouds *over the mountains* today.

They've installed some cabinets *over the counter* in the kitchen.

There are several people *over me* in the chain of command.

The workers don't like the new supervisor who's been put *over them.*

The temperature didn't go *over freezing* all day.

A closely related meaning of **over** is *above and to the other side of.*

The dog jumped *over the fence.*

I can't see *over the wall.*

He threw the ball right *over the house.*

Another related meaning of **over** is *so as to cover* or *covering*.

She put her hand *over her mouth.*
He had a mask *over his face.*

Over can also mean *here and there, at one place or another.*

He roamed *over the world* for many years before he settled down.

With *all*, **over** can mean *throughout, at every place in or on.*

There are books *all over his house.*
After the pipe broke, there was water *all over the floor.*
She spread the papers *all over her desk.*
They traveled *all over Europe* last summer.

Over also can mean **across**, both in the sense of *from one side to the other* and in the sense of *on the other side of.*

You have to go *over the railroad tracks* to get to the highway.
There's a pretty little town just *over the border.*

Over can also mean *more than.*

The meeting lasted *over an hour.*
The repairs cost *over a hundred dollars.*
There were *over fifty people* in the room.
We still have *over a mile* to go.

In time expressions, **over** means *during or through a period of time.*

I'm going to get some rest *over the weekend.*
They've become very close friends *over the years.*
We're not planning to go anywhere *over the holidays.*

Over also means *up to and including a particular time.*

I'll be in New York *over Christmas*, but after that I'm going to Florida.
She'll stay with us *over the weekend*, but then she has to leave.

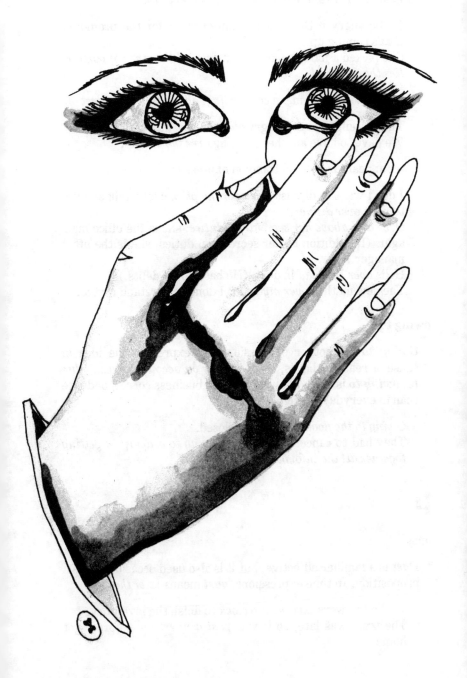

She put her hand *over her mouth*.

Still another meaning of **over** is *in preference to*.

I'll be angry if they choose him *over me* for the promotion that's coming up.
She picked a job in a small town *over all the other opportunities that she had.*

Over is also used to mean *concerning, about, on the subject of*.

The citizens are very angry *over the new taxes.*
We have to have another meeting *over the budget.*

Over appears in several common expressions.

I don't want to discuss this *over the phone;* let's talk about it tonight *over dinner.*
Over and above her secretarial duties, she is the office manager. (In addition to her secretarial duties, she is the office manager.)
He is *over his head* in debt. (He has a lot of debts.)
The new math is *over my head;* I don't understand it at all.

owing to

Owing to is another expression that expresses the idea of cause or reason, that is, *because of* or *on account of*. Like **due to**, **owing to** is more likely to occur in business correspondence than in everyday speech.

Owing to the flood, the road is closed.
They had to cancel the meeting *owing to a delay in getting together all the information they needed.*

p

past

Past is a familiar adjective, but it is also used occasionally as a preposition. In time expressions, **past** means *later than*.

We had to work *past nine o'clock* to finish the inventory.
The train was late, so it was *past dinnertime* before I got home.

In place expressions, **past** means *farther on than*.

My house is just *past the next corner*.
I think we've gone *past the corner where we should have turned*.

Past also has the same meaning as **beyond** in the sense of *outside* or *too much for understanding*, etc.

I don't know how you could have made so many mistakes. It's *past belief!*

per

Per is another Latin word that has been taken into English. One of its meanings is *for each one*.

This wire costs a dollar *per foot*.
The speed limit is 55 miles *per hour*.
His car will get 30 miles *per gallon* on the highway.

The use of **per** in this sense is widespread, as witness the common abbreviation *mph* for *miles per hour*. Many grammarians, however, prefer the use of **a** or **an** because **per** is a borrowed, rather than a native, English word.

Per is also used—usually in business correspondence or similar usage—in the sense of *according to* or *by the terms of*. It is sometimes preceded by *as*.

We wish to remind you that payment is overdue *per our agreement of July 19*.
They sent the merchandise by air *as per the customer's request*.

in place of

In place of, like **instead of**, is used to express the idea of substitution or replacement.

I studied Spanish *in place of Italian* because all the Italian classes were filled.
They're going to put up an office building *in place of those nice old houses*.

69

plus

Plus is a Latin word meaning *more*. It is used in English in formulas for addition or to mean *in addition to*. It is the opposite of *minus*.

Twelve plus seven is nineteen. (12 + 7 = 19.)
You have to finish the report *plus all these letters* today.

r

re

Re is still another Latin word which is sometimes roughly translated as *about the thing*. It is used in English to mean *on the subject of* or *in the case of*. Its use is generally confined to legal documents, business correspondence, or similar uses. It is sometimes combined with *in* to form the phrase *in re* with the same meaning as *re*.

Re our telephone conversation, I want to confirm our agreement to deliver your shipment by October 10.
We have a number of questions *in re our contract with you*.

in reference to
in/with regard to
regarding
as regards

All of these expressions have the meaning of *about, concerning, on the subject of*. They are more likely to occur in business correspondence or similar uses than in everyday speech.

In reference to our agreement of January 8, 1982, I wish to point out that I have not received the payment that was scheduled for the first quarter of this year.
We haven't reached any decision *in regard to the matter that we were discussing yesterday*.
With regard to your résumé, we will keep it on file until such time as there is an appropriate vacancy.
They're having a meeting *regarding some legal problems that have arisen*.

As regards the other items on the agenda, we'll have to postpone discussing them until our next meeting.

regardless of

Regardless of means *without thinking about* or *without considering the expense, danger*, etc.

He's going ahead and building his dream house *regardless of the money he'll have to spend.*
They're going to organize an expedition to climb the mountain *regardless of its reputation as a man-killer.*
I'm going to let the boss know what I think about the new procedures *regardless of the consequences.*

respecting

Respecting is another of the prepositions that is used primarily in business correspondence, etc., to mean *about, concerning, on the subject of.*

He's preparing to make a statement to the press *respecting his candidacy.*

round

Round has all the same meanings as **around**; that is, it can mean *encircling, on all sides of, here and there*, etc. **Around**, however, is much more common in all these senses, though **round** is preferred in formal usage to mean *encircling*.

She had a ribbon tied *round her hair.*
They've just opened the new highway that goes *round the city.*

S

save

Save is one of the prepositions of exclusion like **but** and **except**. In modern usage, **save** is essentially a literary word.

Everyone was rescued *save the captain of the ship.*

71

since

Since is a preposition of time that indicates the beginning point of an action. The action can be either continuous or one which has happened at one time or another within the period.

I've been living here *since the end of 1980.*
She's called me twice *since Sunday.*

Since should only be used with present perfect or past perfect verb phrases.

We've discussed the matter several times *since the meeting.*
I hadn't seen her *since July.*

Since is often contrasted with **for**, which indicates the duration of an action rather than the point of time at which it began.

They've been working on the budget *since Monday.*
They've been working on the budget *for the whole week.*
We've been having extremely cold weather *since Christmas.*
We've been having extremely cold weather *for several weeks.*

in spite of

In spite of is a common prepositional expression used to indicate contrast or opposition. It occurs more frequently than *despite* in everyday speech.

He got the job *in spite of his lack of experience.*
She's been very successful *in spite of all the difficulties that she's encountered in the business world.*
They're going ahead with the project *in spite of all the public protests against it.*
We still swim in the river *in spite of the pollution.*

t

than

Than is one of the most common words in English because of its use in comparisons. In that use, it is classified as a conjunction, even though many of the clauses that follow it are shortened so that they resemble prepositional phrases. However, **than** is used as a preposition meaning *compared with* before *whom* or *which*. Note that this is a very formal and literary usage.

She's an administrator *than whom* there's none better. (She's a better administrator than anybody else.)

It was a period of his life *than which* he had never encountered such difficulties. (He encountered more difficulties during this period of his life than during any other.)

through

Through is used with verbs of motion to mean *in one side and out the other* or *from one end to the other.*

She's coming *through the door* now.

We had to drive all the way *through the city* to get to the highway.

I walk *through the park* every day on my way to work.

We'll be going *through Phoenix* in June; we can see you then.

I've been *through the city*, but I've never had time to stop and do any sightseeing.

Through is used as a time expression to mean *from the beginning to the end*. It answers the question *How long?* rather than *When?*

How long did you sleep on Sunday?

I slept *through the whole morning.*

How long did the child sit without speaking?

She sat *through the entire puppet show* without saying a word.

Through is also used in expressions of manner with the meanings of *by means of, as a result of, because of.*

She's educated herself *through her own efforts.*

I learned everything I know *through reading every book I could get my hands on.*

He's succeeded *through hard work*.
I got my job *through a friend*.

throughout

In time expressions, **throughout** is more emphatic than **through** in conveying the idea of an entire period of time.

It rained *throughout the weekend*.
We had to work *throughout the night* to get the shipment ready.
We'll be interviewing job applicants *throughout the month of October*.

Throughout is also used in place expressions to mean *in every part of, everywhere in*.

They're making changes *throughout the company*.
There's a great deal of new construction *throughout the city*.
There will be thunderstorms *throughout the area* over the weekend.

till

Till is a short form for *until*. See *until* for all uses of both these words.

to

To is used with verbs of motion to indicate the direction or the point where the action ends.

We went *to a movie* last night.
We walked *to the theater*.
They're moving *to Florida* next month.
I drove *to my friend's house*.
She's planning a trip *to South America*.
They transferred him *to the accounting department*.
She sent me *to the post office*.
An ambulance took him *to the airport*.
You can take an express elevator *to the 40th floor*.

We walked *to the theater*.

To is used in time expressions with minutes before the hour.

> It's *five minutes to eight.*
> I'll meet you at *a quarter to nine.*
> I went out to lunch at *twenty-five to one.*
> I got to the doctor's office at *ten to three.*

To also expresses the time an action ends when the time the action begins is given with *from.*

> I have to work *from eight to four* next week.
> We're going to be off *from Friday to Tuesday.*
> Her vacation is *from the last week in July to the second week in August.*

To has two very important functions. The first is to signal the infinitive.

> They want to find a larger house.
> We have to finish the report today.
> I used to live in New York.
> She asked me to come for dinner next Friday.

All prepositions except **to** are followed by the present participle—the *-ing* form—rather than the simple form of the verb.

> You must lock the door *on leaving* the house.
> We haven't made such progress *toward achieving* our goals.
> He was surprised *at getting* a promotion.
> She's counting *on getting* a raise next month.

There are a few expressions in which **to** is followed by the present participle instead of the simple form of the verb.

> I couldn't get used *to working* in a factory.
> She wasn't used *to driving* in the city.
> He won't ever admit *to making* a mistake.
> You have to stick *to studying* if you're going to pass your exams.
> We'll be looking forward *to seeing* you when we're in the city.

The second functional use of **to** is to introduce a prepositional phrase that acts as a substitute for an indirect object.

She handed me a magazine.
She handed a magazine *to me*.
They're going to give us the money next week.
They're going to give the money *to us* next week.
You have to send them the bill of lading today.
You have to send the bill of lading *to them* today.

In American usage, the prepositional phrase is always used when both direct and indirect objects are personal pronouns.

She handed it *to me*.
They haven't returned them *to us* yet.
I've already sent it *to them*.

on top of

On top of means *at the uppermost level of.*

They're installing a TV antenna *on top of the building.*
I put my letter *on top of all the other papers* on her desk.

On top of is also occasionally used to mean *in addition to.*

On top of all his troubles at work, he had an automobile accident last week.

toward

When used with verbs of motion, **toward** indicates the general direction without stating whether the place of destination is actually reached. **To**, however, gives the exact direction or the point where the action ends.

She had started *toward the door* when I called her back.
The storm was coming *toward us* rapidly.
He was smiling as he came *toward me*.
They were walking slowly *toward the house*.
He's working *toward his degree* in electrical engineering.
We're moving *toward greater efficiency* in our manufacturing operations.

Toward is used in time expressions to mean *approaching or just before a certain time.*

It started to rain *toward sunrise.*
Christopher Columbus discovered America *toward the end of the fifteenth century.*
The plane should arrive *toward nine o'clock.*

Toward can also mean *facing.*

We didn't see her because she was standing with her back *toward us.*

Toward can also be used to mean **concerning** or **about**.

I think the boss's feelings *toward me* are good.

Toward can also express purpose in the sense of anticipating or contributing to something in the future.

He's started saving money *toward the time* when he retires.

towards

Towards is usually considered the equivalent of **toward**. In other words, the two prepositions can be used interchangeably. There are some grammarians, however, who consider the use of **towards** to be non-standard.

u

under

Under is another common preposition with a number of different meanings, many of which are the opposite of **over**. Whereas **over** means *at a higher level in place, authority, degree,* etc., **under** means *at a lower level.*

There's a light *over his desk.*
His books are *under his desk.*
It's shady and cool *under these trees.*
I have several people working *under me.*
She didn't like working *under another woman.*
The temperature stayed *under freezing* all day.

Under also means *below and to the other side.*

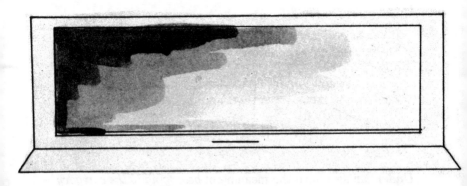

His books are *under his desk*.

You have to go *under the bridge* before you turn onto the highway.

Under also has the general meaning of *covered or hidden by, beneath the surface of.*

It was so cold last night that I slept *under several blankets.*
She couldn't find the letter because it was *under so many other papers.*
I wore a sweater *under my coat,* but I still felt cold.
There is solid rock *under this thin layer of topsoil.*

A related meaning is *in the character of* or *disguised by.*

He got a license *under a false name.*

Under can also have the meaning of *belonging to the category of.*

You should file those letters *under "Pending Business."*

Under can also mean *in the state or act of, in the process of.*

There are several buildings *under construction.*
The elevator is *under repair.*
They haven't reached a decision; the matter is still *under discussion.*
You are *under contract* with us; you can't work for them.
Under law, they're not liable for the damages.
You'll have to swear to the truth *under oath.*

Under is also used in the sense of *at the time of.*

England prospered *under Henry VIII and Elizabeth I.*

Still another meaning of **under** is *authorized by.*

They started to carry out the new policies on the basis of a letter *under the president's signature.*

Under is also used in several familiar expressions.

He can't leave school because he's *under age.*
I know you weren't feeling well; *under the circumstances,* you did quite well on the exam.

I was *under the impression* she was coming with you.
I'm feeling a little *under the weather* today; I'm tired and I have a headache.

underneath

Underneath combines *under* and *beneath* in another preposition with the general meaning of *at a lower level than* or *hidden or concealed below*.

She keeps her sweaters in a box *underneath her bed*.
I found my keys *underneath a pile of clothes*.
They're going to build a garage *underneath the park*.
She doesn't want to work *underneath anyone else*; she wants to have a business of her own so she can be completely independent.

unless

Unless is used principally as a conjunction with the conditional meaning of *if not*, but it is occasionally used as a preposition of exclusion like *except* or *but*. This is a very formal and literary usage.

Nothing will result from the new regulations *unless complete confusion*.

until/till

Until is a common preposition with the meaning of *up to the time of* or *before a particular time*. *Till* is the short form of *until*.

I have to stay *until six o'clock this evening*.
She'll be in school *until June this year*.
He won't be back *until late tonight*.
You have *till Friday* to finish your thesis.
I didn't get to bed *until midnight*.

When *from* is used to indicate the time an action begins, *until* or *till* are used to indicate the time an actions ends.

I worked *from three o'clock until midnight* Wednesday.
She'll be gone *from Tuesday till Thursday*.

Till, but rarely *until*, is used instead of *to* or *of* for minutes before the hour.

> I got to the office at *five minutes to eight.*
> I got to the office at *five minutes of eight.*
> I got to the office at *five minutes till eight.*
> The store will open at *a quarter to ten.*
> The store will open at *a quarter of ten.*
> The store will open at *a quarter till ten.*

up

Up occurs most commonly as an adverb. It also occurs as a preposition with verbs of motion to mean *from a lower to a higher level.*

> We have to walk *up a steep hill* to get to school.
> You have to climb *up these steps* to get to the third floor.

In the expression *up river*, **up** signifies *toward the source of the river.* In the expression *up country*, **up** signifies *toward the interior.* See **down** for the difference between **up** and **down** in giving directions.

upon

Upon can be substituted for all the uses of *on* except with the names of streets and the days of the week, the months, and the names of holidays. *Upon*, however, is a much more formal and literary expression. It seldom occurs in everyday speech.

> I first met him *upon a dark and stormy day.*
> They were standing *upon the deck of the ship* when they saw the dolphins playing in the sea.

V

versus

Versus, often abbreviated *vs.*, is another Latin preposition which has been taken into English. It means *against* and it oc-

We have to walk *up a steep hill* to get to school.

curs most often in the two very different fields of sports and law.

> Pittsburgh *versus Dallas* should be an exciting football game.
> The case of the People *versus O'Malley* will come to trial next week.
> Wykoff *vs. Graham* is the third case on this morning's docket.
> We have to weigh the assets of the company *versus its liabilities* before we decide whether or not to invest in it.

via

Via is still another Latin word which serves as an English preposition. It means *by way of* or *passing through*.

> She went from New York to San Francisco *via Chicago*.
> The main highway is blocked, but you can get to town *via a back road*.

In a rather non-standard usage, *via* can also mean *by means of*.

> I've read all of Lorca's plays *via English translations*.
> She sent the letter to Argentina *via air mail*.

in view of

In view of is another phrase that expresses the idea of cause or reason.

> *In view of his deteriorating health*, he shouldn't be working at all.
> *In view of our rising costs*, we're going to have to consider increasing our prices.

W

wanting

Wanting is used as a preposition in the sense of *lacking* or *without*. It is a very rare literary expression.

She sent us the manuscript of her novel *wanting the final chapter*.

by way of

By way of is a much more common phrase for expressing the same idea as ***via***.

They're planning to go to Florida *by way of Washington*.
That flight doesn't go direct; it goes *by way of Atlanta*.

with

With is another of the high-frequency prepositions with a number of different meanings. One of its principal uses is to express the idea of accompaniment—*accompanied by* or *in the company of*.

I take a long walk *with my dog* every night after dinner.
She's going to be traveling *with the president of the corporation*.
He dropped by last night *with a lot of his friends*.
They always travel *with a lot of baggage*.

In the sense of accompaniment, ***with*** can also carry the additional meaning of *at the same time as*.

He always has coffee *with his dessert*.
Rain usually comes *with a sudden change in the direction of the wind*.

With can also mean *in the same direction as*.

They've increased the speed of travel by flying *with the prevailing winds*.

With also has several uses that indicate some kind of interaction.

Come here and sit *with me*.
The children like to play *with the cat*.
Carol is in love *with Mark*.
I don't like to deal *with that store*; the quality isn't good and the prices are too high.

She's been talking *with all the employees* about their suggestions for improving working conditions.

His rent is so high that he's looking for someone to share the apartment *with him.*

I agree *with you* completely; I think you're a hundred percent right.

I hope you'll side *with me* on this issue; I need your support.

You can mix red *with blue* to make purple.

She always mixes *with the other guests* at a party.

They're always comparing my work *with hers,* but it isn't fair because she's had a lot more experience than I have.

With is also used to show instrument or means.

She stirred all the ingredients *with a wooden spoon.*

He fastened the picture to the wall *with a nail.*

I can't unlock the door *with this key.*

She wouldn't accept his homework because he'd written it *with a pencil.*

In is also used to indicate instrument, but in that case the article is omitted.

She wouldn't accept his homework because he'd written it *in pencil.*

You have to sign your name *in black ink.*

I like to paint *in watercolors.*

On is occasionally used to express instrument.

She always writes all her letters directly *on the typewriter.*

She played me a new song *on her piano.*

With is often followed by the name of a material.

The kitchen counter is covered *with plastic.*

Bronze is an alloy of copper mixed *with tin.*

The balloon was filled *with hot air,* not *with helium.*

With is frequently used in expressions of manner, those which answer the question *How?*

How does he do his work?

She stirred all the ingredients *with a wooden spoon*.

He always does it *with great care.* (He always does it very carefully.)
How did they react to the good news?
They reacted *with joy.* (They reacted joyously.)
How did she solve the problem?
She solved it *with ease.* (She solved it easily.)
How did she accept the prize?
She accepted it *with pleasure.*
How does he feel about his new assignment?
He's looking forward to it *with satisfaction.*

Another important meaning of **with** is *characterized by* or *identified by.*

It's the house *with the big front porch.*
The manager is the woman *with the gray hair.*
People *with pleasant personalities* often get ahead easily.

With sometimes expresses the idea of cause, reason, or result.

He was weak *with hunger.*
A lot of children stay out of school *with colds* during the winter.

With can also mean *in proportion to.*

His ability to make decisions has increased *with experience.*
I hope I'm growing more tolerant *with age.*

With can also be used to mean *about* or *concerning.*

I was very happy *with the results of the elections.*
She's pleased *with her new assignment.*

Still another meaning of **with** is *in the care of.*

Leave the letters *with me*; I'll see that they get to the post office before the last pick-up.
The children stayed *with my parents* while we were on vacation.

With is also used to express support or agreement.

I certainly do agree *with you*; I think you're absolutely right.

It's the house *with the big front porch.*

All the members of the club were *with me* on the new rules.
(They all supported or agreed with me.)
Whoever isn't *with us* is against us.

With can also mean just the opposite, that is, *against, in opposition to, in competition with.*

He's always arguing *with all the other people in the office.*
I don't want to fight *with anyone.*
You don't have to compete *with me.* I'm sure we'll both get our promotions.

With also expresses the idea of separation.

He doesn't like to part *with any of his possessions.*

With is also occasionally used with the same meaning as *in spite of.* It is usually followed by *all* in this sense.

With all his talents, he's never been very successful.

With also occurs in several familiar expressions.

What's the matter *with you*? You look terrible today.
I don't know what's wrong *with the baby.* She's been crying all day.
We think Joan is going *with Bill.* They've been out on five dates this week.
Does this green blouse go *with my red skirt*?

within

Within is similar in meaning to **inside**, with the added idea of *in the inner part of.* This is a rather literary usage.

He had hidden the document *within a bundle of old letters.*
There are hundreds of hiding places *within the castle.*

Within also has the additional idea of *inside the limits or limitations of time, space, degree,* etc., or *inside a limited group.*

There were a few gardens and orchards *within the city walls.*
You must perform your duties *within the rules and regulations* that have been established for your job.

There have been many advances in technology *within my lifetime*.

There's been a lot of tension *within the family* lately.

There have been rumors about a power struggle *within the top management group of the corporation*.

Within has the negative meaning of *not beyond in time, space, degree*, etc.

She was still *within sight* while I was waving goodbye.

You must learn to live *within your income*.

If he'd kept *within the law*, he wouldn't be in prison.

My house is *within a mile of the center of the city*.

I'll have this proposal for you *within a week*.

He claims that he's *within a year of achieving his financial goals*.

I was *within one point of a perfect score*.

without

Without is frequently used as a negative for **with**. In this sense, it has the meaning of *in the absence of* or *lacking*.

You can't leave *without permission from your supervisor*.

I can't eat this ice cream *without a spoon*.

He's traveling *without any baggage*.

You can't get a room in the hotel *without an advance reservation*.

We'll have to begin the meeting *without the absent members*.

A related meaning of **without** is *free from*.

That child is completely *without fear*.

He answered all the questions *without hesitation*.

I know that this machine is going to work *without any difficulty*.

Without also conveys the idea of avoiding something or failing to do something. Note the use of the present participle that follows the preposition **without**.

She was so angry that she walked out *without saying goodbye*.

He left *without cleaning up his desk.*

Without is occasionally used to mean **outside**, usually in opposition to **within**.

There was a good water supply both *within and without the city walls.*

Without can often be understood in a negative conditional sense.

I can't go ahead with this project *without better instructions.* (If I don't get better instructions, I can't go ahead with this project.)
I don't feel well *without eight hours' sleep* every night. (If I don't get eight hours' sleep every night, I don't feel well.)

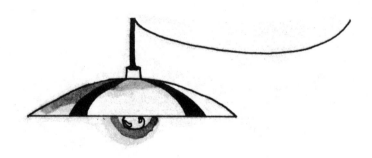

He left *without cleaning up his desk.*